COMMUNITY HELPERS

Veterinarians

by Christina Leaf

BLASTOFF! READERS

BELLWETHER MEDIA • MINNEAPOLIS, MN

Note to Librarians, Teachers, and Parents:

Blastoff! Readers are carefully developed by literacy experts and combine standards-based content with developmentally appropriate text.

Level 1 provides the most support through repetition of high-frequency words, light text, predictable sentence patterns, and strong visual support.

Level 2 offers early readers a bit more challenge through varied simple sentences, increased text load, and less repetition of high-frequency words.

Level 3 advances early-fluent readers toward fluency through increased text and concept load, less reliance on visuals, longer sentences, and more literary language.

Level 4 builds reading stamina by providing more text per page, increased use of punctuation, greater variation in sentence patterns, and increasingly challenging vocabulary.

Level 5 encourages children to move from "learning to read" to "reading to learn" by providing even more text, varied writing styles, and less familiar topics.

Whichever book is right for your reader, Blastoff! Readers are the perfect books to build confidence and encourage a love of reading that will last a lifetime!

This edition first published in 2018 by Bellwether Media, Inc.

No part of this publication may be reproduced in whole or in part without written permission of the publisher. For information regarding permission, write to Bellwether Media, Inc., Attention: Permissions Department, 5357 Penn Avenue South, Minneapolis, MN 55419.

Library of Congress Cataloging-in-Publication Data

Names: Leaf, Christina, author.
Title: Veterinarians / by Christina Leaf.
Description: Minneapolis, MN : Bellwether Media, Inc., 2018. | Series: Blastoff! Readers. Community Helpers | Includes bibliographical references and index. | Audience: Ages 5 to 8. | Audience: Grades K to 3.
Identifiers: LCCN 2017032149 (print) | LCCN 2017044601 (ebook) | ISBN 9781626177512 (hardcover : alk. paper) | ISBN 9781681034522 (ebook)
Subjects: LCSH: Veterinarians–Juvenile literature. | Veterinary medicine–Juvenile literature.
Classification: LCC SF756 (ebook) | LCC SF756 .L428 2018 (print) | DDC 636.089092–dc23
LC record available at https://lccn.loc.gov/2017032149

Editor: Nathan Sommer   Designer: Brittany McIntosh

Printed in the United States of America, North Mankato, MN.

Table of Contents

Cat Calmer

The cat meows loudly. It does not like visits to the veterinarian.

The veterinarian talks softly to the cat. This calms it down. Now the **checkup** can start!

What Are Veterinarians?

Veterinarians are doctors for animals. They are also called vets.

Most vets work in animal **clinics** or **hospitals**. Some travel to farms.

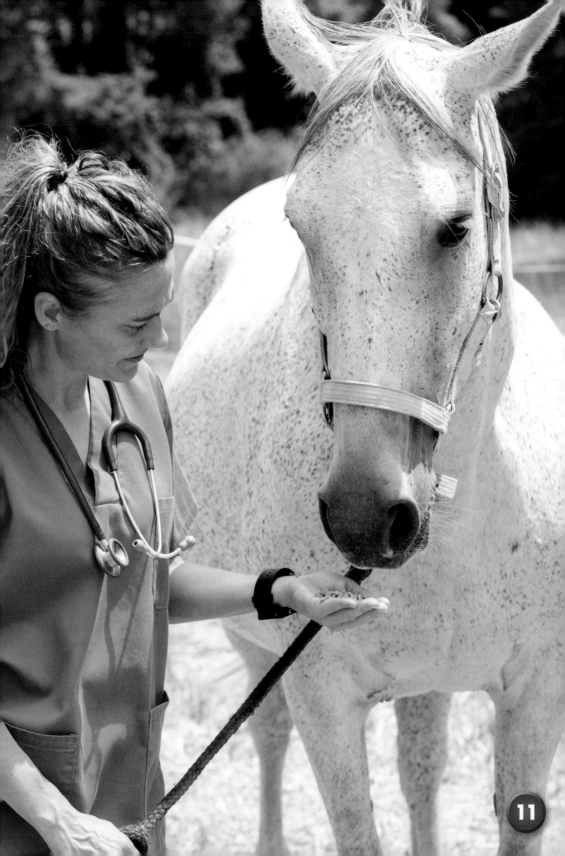

What Do Veterinarians Do?

Vets do checkups on animals. They study their health.

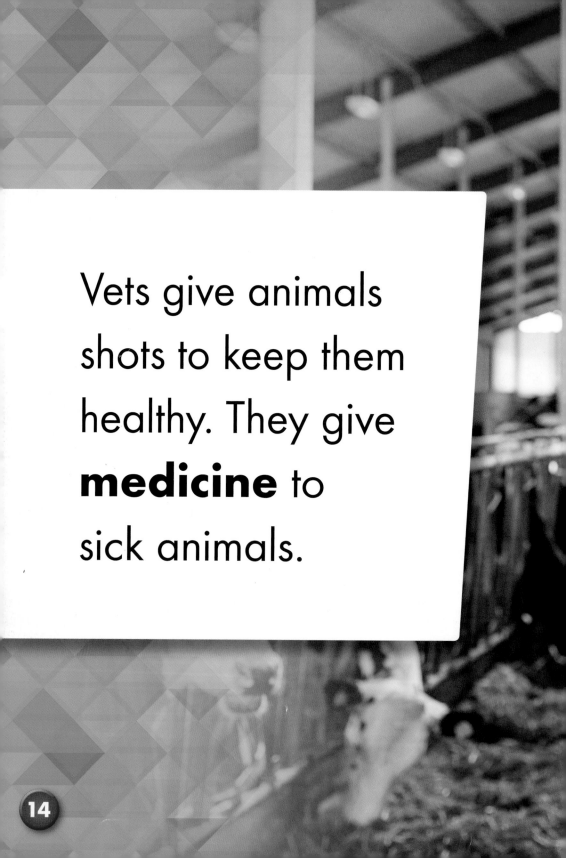

Vets give animals shots to keep them healthy. They give **medicine** to sick animals.

Vets **operate** on hurt animals. They also treat **wounds**.

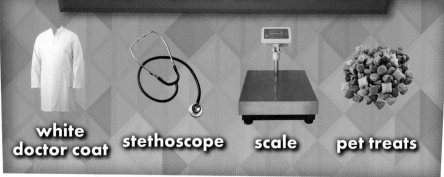

white doctor coat   **stethoscope**   **scale**   **pet treats**

vet operating

17

What Makes a Good Veterinarian?

Vets talk clearly about sickness and care. They help owners understand problems.

Veterinarian Skills

- ✓ gentle
- ✓ caring
- ✓ good communicators
- ✓ problem-solvers

Vet visits can be scary. But vets are caring. They keep animals and owners calm!

Glossary

checkup

a medical visit to check an animal's health

medicine

drugs used to treat sicknesses

clinics

places where animals get checkups and other short medical visits

operate

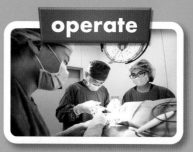

to perform a medical treatment that involves cutting into the body

hospitals

places where animals get emergency care or long medical visits

wounds

places on the body where skin is broken

To Learn More

AT THE LIBRARY

Arnold, Quinn M. *Veterinarians*. Mankato, Minn.: Creative Education, 2017.

Bellisario, Gina. *Let's Meet a Veterinarian*. Minneapolis, Minn.: Millbrook Press, 2013.

Waldendorf, Kurt. *Hooray for Veterinarians!* Minneapolis, Minn.: Lerner Publications, 2017.

ON THE WEB

Learning more about veterinarians is as easy as 1, 2, 3.

1. Go to www.factsurfer.com.

2. Enter "veterinarians" into the search box.

3. Click the "Surf" button and you will see a list of related web sites.

With factsurfer.com, finding more information is just a click away.

Index